POLITICAL LEADERS

ANITA YASUDA

Weigl

Published by Weigl Educational Publishers Limited
6325 10th Street SE
Calgary, Alberta, Canada
T2H 2Z9

Website: www.weigl.com

Library and Archives Canada Cataloguing in Publication data available upon request.
Fax (403) 233-7769 for the attention of the Publishing Records department.

ISBN 978-1-55388-691-4 (hard cover)
ISBN 978-1-55388-696-9 (soft cover)

Printed in the United States of America in North Mankato, Minnesota
1 2 3 4 5 6 7 8 9 0 14 13 12 11 10

072010
WEP230610

All of the Internet URLs given in the book were valid at the time of publication. However, due to the
dynamic nature of the Internet, some addresses may have changed, or sites may have ceased to exist
since publication. While the author and publisher regret any inconvenience this may cause readers, no
responsibility for any such changes can be accepted by either the author or the publisher.

Weigl acknowledges Getty Images, the National Archives of Canada, and the Glenbow
Museum as image suppliers for this title.

Every reasonable effort has been made to trace ownership and to obtain permission to reprint copyright
material. The publishers would be pleased to have any errors or omissions brought to their attention so
that they may be corrected in subsequent printings.

We acknowledge the financial support of the Government of Canada through the Canada Book Fund for
our publishing activities.

EDITOR: Heather Kissock
DESIGN: Terry Paulhus

Since the beginning of the twentieth century, Canada has grown to become a country known for its moderate government, cultural diversity, and active citizenship. Canadian political leaders have moulded the nation through their dreams and statesmanship. They have worked at the municipal, provincial, and federal levels of government to bring about positive change. Many of their decisions, actions, reforms, and accomplishments have improved the quality of life for many Canadians.

In the last 100 years, women have won the right to vote, Medicare has become a national policy, and the rights and freedoms of all Canadian citizens have been protected in the country's Constitution. Canada's reputation for social reform, peacekeeping, and diplomacy has improved both the country and the world.

Canadian leaders worked hard to build the nation. Some of their efforts were symbolic, such as the creation of the Canadian flag and the national anthem. Other efforts were more concrete and included passing laws to protect all citizens and guarantee basic human rights. All of these steps have helped form a unique Canadian identity that is known throughout the country and the world.

As Canada moves into the 21st century, political leaders are making strides to protect the environment and build a respectful relationship with Aboriginal Canadians. Whatever the future holds, Canada's political leaders will continue to shape and develop Canada's national and international profile. The desire to build the best nation possible continues to guide Canada to a brighter future.

Political Leaders
2000s

Farewell Trudeau

Farewell Trudeau

In 2000, Canadians paid their last respects to former Prime Minister Pierre Elliott Trudeau. Crowds gathered by train tracks as his funeral train journeyed from Ottawa to Montreal. People waved Canadian flags, saluted, clapped, and sang "O Canada." Two of Trudeau's most important contributions to Canada were the Official Languages Act, which declared Canada a bilingual country, and the Canadian Charter of Rights and Freedoms, which guaranteed the political and **civil rights** of all Canadian citizens.

2000s

Stockwell Day

In 2000, Stockwell Day became leader of the Canadian Alliance, a right-wing conservative party with strong western Canadian roots. Day, a former preacher, had little national political experience. He was criticized for not campaigning on Sundays, for his opposition to gun control, and for supporting capital punishment. The Canadian Alliance did well in the West but did not break through in Ontario. After the party's defeat in the 2000 federal election, Day said, "The message to us is not yet. Not this time." In 2003,

the Canadian Alliance and the Progressive Conservative Party merged to form the Conservative Party of Canada.

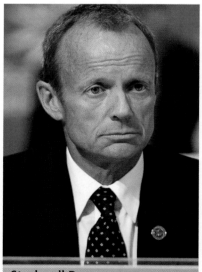

Stockwell Day

2001

Canada hosts the Summit of the Americas.

2002

Stephen Harper defeats Stockwell Day to become leader of the Canadian Alliance.

2003

Paul Martin of the Liberal Party is sworn in as prime minister.

Canadian Forces

In 2001, a terrorist group called Al-Qaeda hijacked airliners and flew them into buildings in the United States. Thousands of people died as a result of these attacks. The United States linked Al-Qaeda to Afghanistan's ruling Taliban government, which was known for its restrictive laws. Canada joined the U.S. and other countries in overthrowing the Taliban. After the Taliban fell in 2001, an International Security Assistance Force (ISAF) was formed to help rebuild the country. **NATO** assumed responsibility for the ISAF in 2003. Canada is one of 46 countries helping the Afghan government establish a stable and secure country. This has proven to be difficult as the Taliban continue to fight against the new government and the NATO led force. With a growing number of casualties, there were calls for Canadian troops to be pulled out of Afghanistan. After much consideration, Prime Minister Harper determined that Canada's future role in Afghanistan should move away from battle and instead place a greater weight on peacekeeping and reconstruction. In the fall election of 2008, Harper said that, in 2011, the majority of Canadian troops would be withdrawn from Afghanistan.

Canadian Forces

2004

Martin's Minority

"Do you want a Canada that builds on its historic strengths and values…?" asked Paul Martin before the 2004 federal election. Voters responded by sending Martin's Liberals to the House of Commons as a minority government. This was Canada's first minority government since 1979. When Martin took office, his main priorities were to implement parliamentary reforms and to increase Canada's visibility on the international stage. However, his term in office was marked by scandal and indecisiveness. Behind the scenes, Martin was often referred to as 'Mr. Dithers' because of his reluctance to make decisions. In the federal election of 2006, Martin lost to the Conservatives. Many blamed the loss on Martin's lack of leadership.

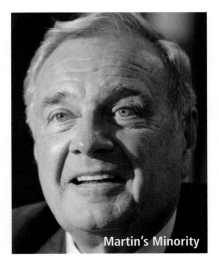

Martin's Minority

2004

Tommy Douglas is voted "The Greatest Canadian" in a CBC poll.

2005

The Liberal government is brought down in a vote of non-confidence.

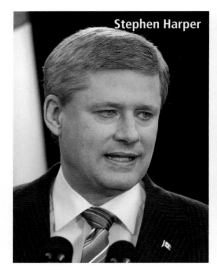
Stephen Harper

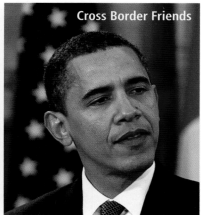
Cross Border Friends

2009

Parliament Shutdown

In December 2009, Prime Minister Harper asked Governor General Michäelle Jean to suspend Parliament until March 2010. The prime minister stated that the government needed time to assess the current economic position and to get the views of constituents on the direction the government should take. The opposition parties viewed the suspension as an escape from controversy. In the months leading up to the shutdown, evidence of human rights abuse of detainees in Afghanistan had come to light. Shutting down Parliament brought an end to the inquiry into the government's role in this situation. As a result, opposition parties accused the government of trying to sabotage the **democratic** process. The governor general granted Harper's request. Parliament did not resume until early March.

2006

Stephen Harper

On January 26, 2006, Stephen Harper became the first Conservative prime minister in 13 years. With only 36 percent of the popular vote, he formed a minority government. One of Harper's first moves as prime minister was to introduce a bill declaring Quebec a nation within a united Canada. This bill was controversial as many Canadians felt that it gave Quebec special status within the country. When it was time to vote, however, Parliament passed the bill. In the next election, in 2008, Harper and the Conservative Party gained more seats in Parliament, but still governed from a minority position.

2009

Cross Border Friends

President Barack Obama's first trip abroad as president of the United States was to Canada. He was so popular with Canadians that a baker in Ottawa even named a pastry after him. Thousands of Canadians turned out to catch a glimpse of President Obama. Obama's visit was seen as important in reducing tensions between the U.S. and Canada over trade, global warming, and the war in Afghanistan.

Parliament Shutdown

2006

Stephen Harper is sworn in as Canada's 22nd prime minister.

2007

Prime Minister Harper announces the creation of a Canadian Museum for Human Rights.

2008

Former students of Aboriginal residential schools are offered an apology by Prime Minister Harper.

Haiti Response

2010 Olympics

Haiti Response

On January 12, 2010, a major earthquake hit Haiti. More than 200,000 people died, and millions of Haitians were left homeless. Canada immediately sent troops, ships, and supplies to provide security and relief. Prime Minister Harper went to Haiti in February 2010, becoming the first **G20** leader to visit that country after the earthquake. While there, Harper announced that Canada would donate $12 million to temporarily house Haitian government departments. The centre of Canadian relief efforts was in Léogâne, a town that was severely damaged in the earthquake.

2010

2010 Olympics

In 2010, Vancouver, British Columbia, hosted the Winter Olympics. This event showcased Canadian athletes and culture to the world. During a speech to the British Columbia legislature, Prime Minister Harper told Canadians to be proud. He said "Canada, our magnificent land, to which we are welcoming the world, not just for the Olympic Games, but as part of our very identity." The theme of the 2010 Opening Ceremony was "to inspire the world." It featured performers such as k.d. Lang and Aboriginal dancers in a show designed to reflect all of Canada's people and traditions. At the first modern Olympic Winter Games in 1924, 16 nations competed. At the 2010 Winter Olympic Games, athletes from 82 nations competed.

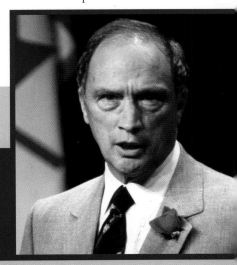

Into the Future

In a poll conducted in the 2000s, Prime Minister Trudeau ranked first as the person who most defined Canada. Do you agree or disagree with this? Can you think of a person, event, or symbol that best represents Canada? What symbol do you think will best represent Canada in the future? Why?

2009

Stephen Harper meets with President Obama in Ottawa on the president's first official trip abroad.

2010

Prime Minister Stephen Harper becomes the first prime minister to address the British Columbian Legislature.

Political Leaders
1990s

The Bloc Québécois as
Official Opposition

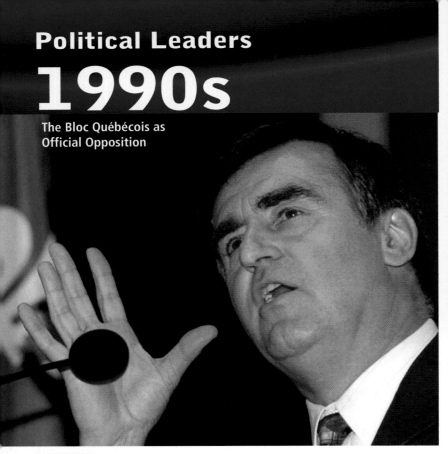

Kim Campbell

1993

Kim Campbell

In nine years, Avril Kim Campbell went from rookie politician in the British Columbia legislature to Minister of National Defence in the federal government. When Brian Mulroney stepped down as leader of the Conservative Party, Campbell ran for the job and won. She automatically became prime minister. This made her the first Canadian woman to hold this position. Campbell was a media sensation. The Conservative Party hoped she could lead them to victory in the next election. It was not to be. The Progressive Conservative Party suffered a defeat to the Liberals. Campbell had been prime minister for almost six months.

1993

The Bloc Québécois as Official Opposition

In the federal election of 1993, the Bloc Québécois, under the leadership of Lucien Bouchard, won enough seats to become the **official opposition** in Ottawa. The Bloc Québécois was a **separatist** party. It ran on a **platform** that supported Quebec leaving Canada. This was the first time in Canadian history that a separatist had become leader of the opposition. Bouchard had not always been a separatist, however. Earlier in his career, he had served as a Cabinet minister under Prime Minister Brian Mulroney. Bouchard's politics changed when the Meech Lake Accord failed. The accord had been an attempt to get Quebec to support the Constitution by giving the province "distinct society" status. When the accord did not pass, Bouchard and several other ministers quit the Conservative Party to form the Bloc Québécois. During the 1993 election, the Bloc Québécois only ran candidates in Quebec. Even so, the party won 54 of the province's 75 ridings. This was enough to make the party the country's official opposition.

1991

Rita Johnston is elected premier of British Columbia, becoming the first female premier in Canada.

1992

The Charlottetown Accord, a package of amendments to Canada's Constitution, is rejected.

Jean Chrétien

"A prime minister has a unique duty .... It is not about power. It is about responsibility," said Jean Chrétien. Chrétien brought a wealth of political experience to the position of prime minister. He was first elected to the House of Commons in 1963. Over the next 17 years, he held every major **portfolio**. In 1990, he won the leadership of the Liberal Party. Chrétien led the Liberals to three consecutive majority governments. Under his tenure as prime minister, there were five budget surpluses, the debt was paid down, and taxes were cut. There were also cuts in federal funding to the provinces. Jean Chrétien retired in 2003 after 40 years in politics.

Jean Chrétien

1995

Jacques Parizeau— Quebec Referendum

When Jacques Parizeau, the premier of Quebec, stated that Quebec would hold a **referendum** to decide whether the province should separate from Canada, shock waves were felt across the country. Canadians wondered if Quebec was really prepared to go its own way. Supporters soon lined up on the **federalist** 'No' side and the separatist 'Yes' side. Prime Minister Chrétien pleaded with Quebecers not to "throw away the dream of Canada."

Lucien Bouchard, who had formed the Bloc Québécois only three years earlier, took a lead role in the 'Yes' campaign. His strong speaking style inspired separatists. It was expected that the referendum was going to be close, and it was. On referendum night, people across Canada anxiously awaited the results. With 50.6 percent of the vote, the 'No' side won. Only 4,288 votes separated the two sides. Premier Parizeau outraged many people when he blamed the loss on "money and the ethnic vote." He then quit as leader of the Parti-Québécois. Alain Nöel, a political science professor said of Parizeau's remarks that, "The **sovereignty** movement has never been so strong – and in a few words, he wiped out that progress.

Jacques Parizeau— Quebec Referendum

1993

Sheila Copps becomes the first woman deputy prime minister.

1994

The Parti Québécois defeats the Liberal Party of Quebec.

1995

Quebec holds a referendum on separation from Canada.

Preston Manning and Reform

2000, the Reform Party had not been able to break through in central or eastern Canada. The party was dissolved and replaced with a new party called the Canadian Alliance in 2000. Stephen Harper became the party's leader. Preston Manning retired from politics and founded the Manning Centre for Building Democracy.

1998

Nisga'a Nation— Joseph Gosnell

As chairman of the Native Brotherhood of British Columbia, Joseph Gosnell championed the rights of First Nations peoples. He came to worldwide attention as the Nisga'a Nation's chief negotiator, when he was able to secure 2,000 square kilometres of the lower Nass Valley, a cash settlement, and legislative power for the Nisga'a Nation through the Nisga'a Treaty. The Nisga'a now had the right to adopt their own constitution and run their own government and police force. Fishing and logging rights in the area were also settled. In return, the Nisga'a gave up the right to future land claims. When the treaty became official, Gosnell said, "This ceremony is a triumph for the Nisga'a people, the people of British Columbia and the people of Canada. Today, we make history as we correct the mistakes of the past and send a signal of hope around the world."

1997

Preston Manning and Reform

A *Globe and Mail* article in 1987 reported that a new party was planning to "put Western concerns on the national agenda." That party was the Reform Party of Canada. Preston Manning, the son of a former Alberta premier, believed his party's support came from the average Canadian. "So you don't trust politicians. Neither do we," was one Reform slogan. In the 1997 federal election, the Reform Party won 60 of 301 seats, making it the official opposition. Many were surprised at how fast the party had grown. However, the growth did not continue. By

Nisga'a Nation—Joseph Gosnell

1996

The Arctic Council is established during a meeting in Ottawa.

1997

The Liberal Party wins a second consecutive majority.

The Creation of Nunavut

In 1976, Inuit leader John Amagoalik travelled to Ottawa to ask Prime Minister Trudeau for treaty recognition and self government. His goal became a reality on May 25, 1993, when the Nunavut land claims agreement was signed. It was the largest Aboriginal land claim settlement in Canadian history. The agreement gave the Inuit title to about 350,000 square kilometres of land. On April 1, 1999, Nunavut became part of Canadian **Confederation**. Of this day, Amagoalik said, "People can no longer talk about Canada being a country founded by two nations. Most people now accept the fact that Canadian history has been a three ways partnership between the English, the French and the Aboriginal people."

Historic Resting Places

Historic Resting Places

In August 1998, Member of Parliament (MP) Roger Gallaway proposed a program to designate the gravesites of former prime ministers as national historic sites. This would mean that they would be conserved and protected for future generations. Many of the gravesites had fallen into disrepair, and Gallaway felt that the sites deserved more respect than they were receiving. His motion quickly gained support. It became known as the National Program for the Grave Sites of Prime Ministers. Today, prime ministers' gravesites across the country fly a Canadian flag, and a plaque is displayed listing the accomplishments of these historic Canadian leaders.

The Creation of Nunavut

Into the Future

Did you know that there are six ways to vote in a federal election? These include a polling station, advance polls, by mail, and in your home in the presence of an election official. Can you think of other ways people might securely cast ballots in future elections?

1998	1999	2000
Joe Clark becomes leader of the Progressive Conservative Party of Canada.	Nunavut becomes Canada's third territory.	Stockwell Day is elected the first leader of the Canadian Alliance Party.

Claude Ryan and the Referendum

Prime Minister Trudeau and the Constitution Act

Until 1982, Canada did not have control over its Constitution. Changes could not be made without permission from the government of Great Britain. On April 17, 1982, Queen Elizabeth II signed into law the Constitution Act of Canada. Canada was now completely independent of Great Britain. Prime Minister Trudeau had been instrumental in achieving this milestone. At the signing ceremony, Trudeau said "Today, at long last, Canada is acquiring full and complete national sovereignty. The Constitution of Canada has come home." The Constitution Act contains the Canadian Charter of Rights and Freedoms. The Charter lists 34 rights and freedoms of Canadian citizens. This includes freedom of speech and religion, the equality of women, and the rights of the disabled. With the exception of Quebec, all Canadian provinces accepted the Constitution.

1980

Claude Ryan and the Referendum

In 1980, Quebec held its first referendum on separating from Canada. During this referendum, Quebec Liberal leader Claude Ryan led the 'No' side. Ryan received support from other well-known federalists, including Prime Minister Trudeau, and Justice Minister Jean Chrétien. The referendum asked Quebecers if Quebec should pursue a path toward independent status. When votes were counted, the 'No' side won 59.56 percent of the vote. Ryan told his supporters that, "We believe it is possible to be proud to be Quebecers and at the same time to be proud of being Canadian." Ryan retired from politics in 1994.

Prime Minister Trudeau and the Constitution Act

1981

An agreement is reached on the patriation of the Constitution.

1982

Bertha Wilson becomes the first woman justice of the Supreme Court.

1983

Brian Mulroney becomes leader of the Progressive Conservative Party.

1982

A Day for Canada

On July 9, 1982, MP Harold Herbert introduced Bill C-201. The House of Commons passed the bill within minutes. The bill officially recognized that the July 1st holiday known as **Dominion** Day would now be called Canada Day. The holiday had been called Dominion Day to mark the creation of the Dominion of Canada under the British North America Act of 1867. The renaming of the holiday was done to show that Canada was now a fully independent country.

1984

John Turner

John Turner had been involved in federal politics since the 1950s. He ran for the Liberal Party leadership in 1968 but lost to Pierre Trudeau. Trudeau made Turner his Minister of Justice and later, his Minister of Finance. Turner served in this position for three years, but he left the job in 1975 to return to his law practice. He returned to politics in 1984, when he ran for leadership of the Liberal Party. When he won the leadership, he automatically became prime minister. Turner immediately called for a federal election, expecting to continue the Liberals' 16-year reign with an easy win. However, he inherited problems from Trudeau's leadership. Under Trudeau, 216 Liberals had been named to government positions, making a clear case for accusations of **patronage**. The Conservative Party leader, Brian Mulroney, used this to his advantage during live television debates, turning the polls in his favour. In the 1984 federal election, Turner was defeated. He had served as prime minister for only 79 days.

A Day for Canada

John Turner

1984

Prime Minister Pierre Trudeau resigns and retires from politics.

1985

Prime Minister Mulroney and U.S. President Reagan meet at the Shamrock Summit in Quebec City.

Brian Mulroney

1984

Brian Mulroney

In 1984, Brian Mulroney won a landslide election to become Canada's 18th prime minister. Mulroney's tenure as prime minister is notable for its efforts to build relations between Canada and the United States. In 1985, Mulroney hosted U.S. President Ronald Reagan at a meeting in Quebec City. The conference was nicknamed the Shamrock Summit because both leaders were of Irish decent. The meeting was productive. The leaders signed a Pacific Salmon Treaty, which ended a dispute about fishing rights along the west coast. Both countries also pledged to improve the Distant Early Warning Line, a network of radar stations that span the Alaskan and Canadian Arctic. The two leaders also agreed to eliminate barriers to trade between the two countries.

1987

Elijah Harper

In 1987, Prime Minister Mulroney met with provincial leaders at Meech Lake, Quebec. They were there to discuss changes to the Constitution. In 1982, Quebec did not accept the Constitution Act. Quebec was now willing to sign the Constitution if it included a statement that Quebec was a distinct society in Canada and if provincial powers were increased. The premiers agreed to these changes, but they still had to receive approval on the Meech Lake Accord from their legislatures. On June 23, 1990, Elijah Harper, an Aboriginal Canadian and a Member of the Legislative Assembly in Manitoba, stood before the province's Speaker of the House. When asked if would give his approval to the Meech Lake Accord, he simply said "No, Mr.

Speaker." Like many Aboriginal leaders, Harper thought the accord should be changed. He argued that it did not do enough to recognize Aboriginal Peoples in Canada. As a result of his actions that day, the Meech Lake Accord was never approved.

Elijah Harper

1986	1987	1988
The House of Commons selects a new speaker by secret ballot for the first time.	The Reform Party of Canada is founded.	Brian Mulroney wins his second majority government.

Ed Broadbent—
A Voice from the Left

won the leadership of the NDP after Ed Broadbent stepped down. During her time as leader, the NDP made strides at the provincial level. In 1990, Bob Rae became premier of Ontario. In 1991, Mike Harcourt was elected premier of British Columbia. The popularity of the NDP, however, did not extend to the federal front. In the 1993 election, the NDP won only nine seats and lost its official party status in the House of Commons. McLaughlin resigned as leader of the NDP in 1994.

1988

Ed Broadbent—A Voice from the Left

In 1987, the New Democratic Party (NDP) surged in popularity. Ed Broadbent was the leader of the federal NDP at the time. Broadbent was responsible for making the party a force from coast to coast. He spoke out for lower taxes, affordable housing, and higher pensions. Under Broadbent, the NDP had its best showing ever in the 1988 federal election. The party won 43 seats. Broadbent was not happy with the results as it was not enough to give the NDP official opposition status. The next year, she

Broadbent resigned after 14 years as leader of the NDP and 21 years as an MP. He returned to politics in 2004, serving under Jack Layton in the NDP **shadow cabinet** until his retirement in 2005.

1989

Audrey McLaughlin

The 1980s saw many firsts for women in politics. Jeanne Sauvé was appointed the first woman Speaker of the House of Commons. Bertha Wilson became the first woman Justice of the Supreme Court, and Audrey McLaughlin became the first woman to lead a national political party. She

Audrey McLaughlin

Into the Future

A country's constitution is often called its foundation. The Canadian Constitution guarantees citizens the right to vote and the right to be heard by government. Why do you think it is important for a country to have a constitution? How does the Constitution affect your life on a daily basis? What do you think would happen if Canada did not have a Constitution?

1989

Audrey McLaughlin wins the NDP leadership race.

1990

The Bloc Québécois party is formed with Lucien Bouchard as its leader.

Political Leaders
1970s

1970

Jean Chrétien as Indian Affairs Minister

In 1969, several First Nations leaders were invited to Ottawa to meet with Indian Affairs Minister Jean Chrétien. At the meeting, Chrétien introduced the government's proposed policy regarding Aboriginal Peoples. The policy advised that the Indian Act be abolished.

The Indian Act had been established in 1951 as a way to determine who was entitled to live on reserve lands. The Liberal government felt that the standards set out in the act were outdated. It argued that "the separate legal status of Indians…have kept the Indian people apart from and behind other Canadians." While the government saw this new policy as a way for First Nations to fully participate in Canadian society,

it was really calling for their **assimilation**. If implemented, the policy would have led to the termination of treaties and any other special status granted to First Nations. The First Nations were opposed to this policy and drafted their official reaction in the document titled *Citizens Plus*, or the *Red Paper*, of 1970. First Nations were interested in self-government and not assimilation, the document explained. Trudeau's government was forced to back down. This was seen as an important victory for Canada's First Nations.

Jean Chrétien as Indian Affairs Minister

1971

Prime Minister Trudeau introduces the Canadian

1972

Joey Smallwood, premier of Newfoundland, retires after 22 years in office.

1973

The Parti Québécois becomes the official

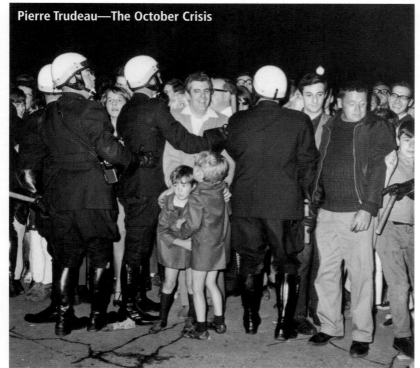

Pierre Trudeau—The October Crisis

Bill Davis

From 1971 until 1985, Ontario was led by Bill Davis of the Progressive Conservative Party. Davis, the 18th premier of Ontario, was the province's second-longest serving premier. He is best remembered for expanding Ontario's public health and bilingual services. He made changes to the Ontario Human Rights Code and the province's education system. Davis felt children should be encouraged and challenged in a less disciplined environment. Under the new curriculum guidelines, children were allowed to choose their own programs and work at their own pace. Davis created two universities and 22 community colleges. He also approved full funding of Ontario's Roman Catholic schools and provided people with better access to student loans.

1970

Pierre Trudeau—The October Crisis

On October 5, 1970, Canadians were shocked to hear that British trade commissioner James Cross had been kidnapped by the Front de libération du Québec (FLQ). The FLQ was a **nationalist** group that believed in using terrorism to achieve its goals. Five days later, the group kidnapped Quebec's minister of labour and immigration, Pierre Laporte. Thus began Quebec's October Crisis. Prime Minister Trudeau did not believe in negotiating with the FLQ. Instead, he invoked the War Measures Act, which suspended **civil liberties**. Soldiers could now patrol the streets looking for the kidnappers. This was the first time in Canadian history that the act had been used during peacetime. Cross was later released unharmed, but Laporte was found dead.

Bill Davis

1974

1975

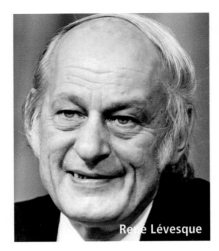

René Lévesque

1976

René Lévesque

From 1976 until 1985, René Lévesque served as premier of Quebec. His separatist party worked for an independent Quebec within an economic union with the rest of Canada. He called this "sovereignty-association." Under Lévesque, the Quebec government passed Bill 101, Charter of the French Language Law. Its purpose was to protect French language and culture. Bill 101 made French the only official language of the province. As a result of the bill, several businesses, including Sun Life Insurance Company, moved their operations out of Quebec. The company was one of the largest employers in Montreal, and the move caused the government to alter the bill. Allowances were then made for the use of English in head offices and in out-of-province communications.

1977

Willie Adams

"It took me about a year to learn the ropes," said Willie Adams, the first Inuit to serve in the Senate. Appointed by Prime Minister Trudeau, Adams served as senator for the Northwest Territories until the creation of Nunavut in 1999. He sat on various Senate committees, including those for the environment and natural resources, Aboriginal affairs, and fisheries.

1979

Who is Joe?

When Joe Clark was chosen leader of the Conservative Party in 1976, few Canadians knew who he was. Newspapers labelled him "Joe Who?" Shortly after Clark's win, he declared, "We will not take this nation by storm, by stealth, or by surprise. We will win it by work." He set out to prove the party's work ethic was strong. When voters went to the polls in 1979, Joe Clark and his Conservative Party won the election, forming a minority government. At age 39, Clark became the youngest person to ever become prime minister of Canada. However, his victory was short-lived. Within a few months, opposition MPs had voted against his budget, and Clark was forced to call an election. The Conservatives lost and returned to Parliament as the opposition. Clark's tenure as prime minister lasted only seven months.

Willie Adams

Who is Joe?

1976

Canada hosts the Olympic

1977

Willie Adams becomes the first Inuit

1978

A new Immigration Act promotes

Into the Future

In the 1970s, the FLQ terrorized Quebec. What had once been a "Quiet Revolution" became a deadly and violent one. What are some positive ways a group can make itself heard? What would you do if you wanted the federal government to change a piece of legislation or bring in a new one? How can you contact your MP? Do you think it is possible for one person or for a group of private citizens to effect a change?

ÉCOLE SCHOOL

1979

Nellie J. Cournoyea becomes the first Aboriginal woman to lead a provincial or territorial government.

1980

Jeanne Sauvé is appointed the first female Speaker of the House of Commons.

1960s

Dief the Chief

1960

Dief the Chief

Prime Minister John Diefenbaker led Canada into the 1960s. Internationally, he worked to advance human rights in countries such as South Africa. Nationally, he gave the right to vote in federal elections to Aboriginal Canadians. He felt that national unity could only be realized if Canadian society were based on fairness. In 1960, he introduced the Canadian Bill of Rights. It guarantees the basic rights of all citizens, including freedom of religion and speech. Diefenbaker said that, "…few Canadians will deny that this is not only a first step in the right direction, but a very important first step, and one that will take its place among the outstanding achievements for the maintenance and preservation of human liberty in Canada."

1960s

The Quiet Revolution

Premier Jean Lesage of Quebec told voters in 1962 that "…it's now or never that we must act to become masters in our own home." Lesage did not want Quebec to separate from Canada, but he did want to modernize the province and implement social changes so that the Francophone community was more empowered. Most of the policies and programs he implemented worked to increase Francophone control over the province's economy. Previously, most businesses in the province were owned by Anglophone companies. Under the Lesage government, a Department of Cultural Affairs and Federal-Provincial Relations was created. Lesage also nationalized all private hydroelectric facilities, created the Quebec Pension Plan, and introduced a family allowance program. In order to put his programs into place, he raised taxes and borrowed from the federal treasury. The creation of these programs reduced the dependence that Quebec had on the federal government and made the province more independent. As a result, the Lesage era became known as the "Quiet Revolution." Relations between the Lesage government and the government of Canada were strained during this period.

The Quiet Revolution

1961

Tommy Douglas becomes leader of the New Democratic Party.

1962

Jean Lesage is re-elected in Quebec.

1963

Support for Diefenbaker's Conservative government collapses.

Prime Minister Pearson

1963

Prime Minister Pearson

In 1963, Lester Pearson was elected the 14th prime minister of Canada. Under Pearson, Canada would develop a new flag, a task force on bilingualism, and a new immigration act. Pearson was seen as a prime minister who cared for the needs of every citizen. He created the Canadian Pension Plan and introduced universal Medicare, which provides health care to all Canadians. Pearson retired from politics in 1968 at the age of 71.

1960s

Bilingualism and Biculturalism

On September 9, 1969, the Official Languages Act (OLA) came into effect. The act was based on the recommendations of the Royal Commission of Bilingualism and Biculturalism (RCBB). The RCBB was created by Lester Pearson on July 19, 1963. The commission had studied English and French relations. The OLA established, for the first time, the right of English- and French-speaking Canadians to access federal services in the language of their choice. This applied to federal courts of law, all federal government ministries and departments, and all **Crown corporations**.

Bilingualism and Biculturalism

1964

Canada officially decides not to participate in the Vietnam War.

1965

Prime Minister Lester B. Pearson establishes a new national flag.

Lester Pearson's Flag Debate

1964

Lester Pearson's Flag Debate

Imagine the Canadian flag with a beaver on it and not a red maple leaf. In 1964, debate raged across Canada when Lester Pearson wanted Canada to have a new and unique flag. For nearly a century, Canada's flag had been modelled after a British naval flag. It featured the Union Jack and Canada's coat of arms. Many designs were considered for Canada's new flag. Each had its supporters. Pearson favoured a design with three maple leaves on a white background with a blue bar on each side. He thought the blue symbolized the Pacific and Atlantic Oceans. After much debate, a flag with a single red maple leaf on a white background with two red borders was approved by Parliament. It was flown on February 15, 1965, for the first time as Canada's official flag.

1967

Vive le Québec Libre

Canada's centennial was celebrated in 1967. Celebrations took place from coast to coast. The highlight of the centennial was the World's Fair, or Expo '67, that was held in Montreal. Expo '67 was a symbol of pride for Canadians. People from across the country came to Quebec to see the monorail, glass domes, and international pavilions that were on display. Many world leaders were invited, including the French president, Charles de Gaulle. On July 24, de Gaulle stood at Montreal's City Hall before a huge cheering crowd. During his speech, he said, "Vive le Québec. Vive le Québec Libre!" In saying this, de Gaulle appeared to be promoting Quebec independence. The federal government was angry. Prime Minister Pearson announced that "Canadians do not need to be liberated." De Gaulle cut his trip short and returned to France, but his words had already sent shock waves throughout Canada. More than 1,000 telegrams and hundreds of phone calls were received by Parliament regarding his comments. His speech served to encourage Quebec separatists.

Vive Le Québec Libre

Trudeaumania

1968

First Televised Debate

On June 9, 1968, nine million people turned on their televisions to watch a major event. It was the first nationally-televised political debate in Canada. The debate featured Tommy Douglas of the NDP, Pierre Trudeau of the Liberals, the Conservative Party's Robert Stanfield, and David Réal Caouette of Quebec's Social Credit Rally. As debates in the House of Commons had yet to be televised, the event was a rare chance to watch the leaders talk about the issues facing Canadians. The debate took place in Confederation Hall in the Parliament Buildings in Ottawa.

1968

Trudeaumania

In 1968, Pierre Elliott Trudeau won the leadership of the federal Liberal Party. The next step was to begin campaigning for a Liberal government in Ottawa. No one had seen a politician quite like Trudeau before. He was young, charming, and fluent in French and English. Trudeau appealed to the young and to the old. Trudeaumania hit the country, and thousands of people came to Liberal rallies to hear him speak. Trudeau's star power led his party to victory, and he became Canada's 15th prime minister.

Into the Future

Canada is officially known as a bilingual country, but almost 70 percent of the population are English speaking and only about 23 percent declare French as their first language. As a result, critics have suggested that Canada's official bilingualism is on paper only and not based on fact. Can you communicate in both of Canada's official languages? What evidence do you see of bilingualism in your community?

1969

Pierre Trudeau makes Canada officially bilingual with the Official Languages Act.

1970

Robert Bourassa becomes the youngest premier of Quebec.

1950s

Charlotte Whitton

W.A.C. Bennett

1951

Charlotte Whitton

The 1950s was a decade of change. One of the biggest changes was the role women began playing in politics. In 1951, Charlotte Whitton became Canada's first woman mayor of a major city. Whitton's civic reforms for Ottawa included developing city services, tighter controls on spending, low-cost housing, and pollution control. Whitton was outspoken on the status of women, once saying, "Whatever women do, they must do twice as well as men to be thought half as good. Luckily, this is not difficult." Ottawa voters re-elected her as mayor in 1952, 1954, 1960, and 1962.

1952

W.A.C. Bennett

Thanks to a new voting system in British Columbia called the alternative ballot system, the 1952 election was unlike any other. The new system asked voters to rank candidates in order of preference. It took three weeks to determine who had won. Finally, it was decided that W.A.C. Bennett was the winner, with a minority government. The victory was a feat for Bennett's Social Credit Party. The party had been largely ignored at the beginning of the campaign. Bennett governed British Columbia during a time of prosperity called the "Bennett boom." He ran the province like his hardware store in Kelowna, with tight control over spending. Bennett was known as a showman. One of his best-known stunts in office was shooting a flaming arrow at a barge of gasoline soaked bonds, to symbolize that the province was debt-free. During Bennett's 20 years as premier, he oversaw major construction projects, such as the Great Eastern Pacific Railway, and hydroelectric projects on the Peace and Columbia Rivers. His government invested in new pulp mills and copper mines. Bennett reduced taxes paid by seniors and the less fortunate and expanded the province's universities. People cheered when he began a publicly owned ferry service to Vancouver Island. In 1972, Bennett lost the election to Dave Barrett of the NDP. Bennett retired, and his son took over the Social Credit Party.

1951

Thérèse Casgrain is chosen as head of the Quebec Co-operative Commonwealth Federation (CCF).

1952

Vincent Massey becomes the first governor general born in Canada.

A Nobel Pearson

1956

A Nobel Pearson

In 1956, a dispute broke out over the Suez Canal, an important shipping route between the Mediterranean Sea and the Red Sea. Lester Pearson, then Secretary of State for External Affairs, was sent to act as Canada's representative at a United Nations meeting to solve the crisis. In order to end the fighting in Egypt, Pearson suggested the creation of a United Nations Emergency Force. The force would oversee peace until a political settlement could be reached. Pearson's idea of a peacekeeping force won favour with the United Nations (UN). It was quickly put into place, and the crisis was settled. In 1957, Pearson was awarded the Nobel Peace Prize for his efforts. On accepting his award he said "I am grateful for the opportunities I have been given to participate in that work as a representative of my country, Canada, whose people have, I think, shown their devotion to peace." Pearson's medal is on display in the lobby of Canada's Foreign Affairs and International Trade headquarters in Ottawa.

1956

Robert Stanfield

Nova Scotia Premier Robert Stanfield earned his nickname "Honest Bob" for his straightforward political style. He is often called the "greatest prime minister Canada never had." Born in Nova Scotia, Stanfield studied economics and political science at Dalhousie University before going to Harvard University, in the United States, to study law. In 1948, he was elected leader of the Conservative Party of Nova Scotia. The party was not popular in the province. It would take him years to improve its reputation. His efforts paid off, when, in 1956, Stanfield led the Conservative Party to victory in the provincial election. He would be re-elected premier of the province four times. While in office, Stanfield brought in reforms in education, municipal government, and health care. He also attracted investment to the province from large international companies, such as Michelin Tires. Later, he moved on to federal politics, becoming the leader of the country's Conservative Party. He resigned from this position in 1976 and retired from politics entirely in 1979.

Robert Stanfield

1953

Prime Minister Louis St. Laurent creates the Department of Northern Affairs.

1954

Louis St. Laurent departs on a global goodwill trip.

1955

Saskatchewan celebrates its 50th anniversary as a province.

John George Diefenbaker

In 1957, John Diefenbaker led the Conservative Party to victory in the federal election, but only as a minority government. The following year, Diefenbaker asked Governor General Georges Vanier to dissolve Parliament. Another election was set for March 31, 1958. Diefenbaker campaigned across Canada. He spoke of his vision for Canada's future, one that included the development of Canada's North and a new national policy in which the basic rights and freedoms of all Canadians would be guaranteed. When the Canadian public went to the polls, they chose Diefenbaker. His Progressive Conservative Party won 208 out of the 265 seats in the House of Commons. This was the largest majority government in Canadian history at the time.

John George Diefenbaker

1956	**1957**	**1958**
Lester Pearson suggests the creation of a United Nations Emergency Force.	The Conservative Party forms a minority government.	James Gladstone becomes Canada's first Aboriginal senator.

Ellen Fairclough

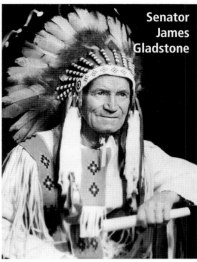

Senator James Gladstone

1957

Ellen Fairclough

Ellen Fairclough, from Hamilton, Ontario, was the first female member of Cabinet. She was first elected to the House of Commons in 1950 and remained the only woman MP until the 1953 election. Prime Minister Diefenbaker appointed her Secretary of State for Canada. She later became his Minister of Citizenship and Immigration. Fairclough was known to be articulate, approachable, and always multitasking. Fairclough was an MP for 13 years. During that time, she averaged 150 speeches a year. Some of her interests included housing, income tax, and the status of women. Fairclough introduced bills to eliminate racial discrimination in immigration policy.

1958

Senator James Gladstone

In 1958, James Gladstone became the first Aboriginal senator. His appointment came two years before Status Indians won the right to vote. As a senator, Gladstone served as co-chairman of a joint Senate–Commons committee on Indian affairs. Prior to his appointment, Gladstone had served as president of the Indian Association of Alberta. He had travelled to Ottawa several times to ask for improvements to the Indian Act. The act defined who an "Indian" was and their legal rights and freedoms. Gladstone worked to increase awareness of Canadian Aboriginal Peoples and their place in society.

Into the Future

The 1950s saw women take great strides in Canadian politics. This progress has continued into the present, with women extending their knowledge and abilities into other fields. Are there any fields that women are still restricted from entering? What can be done to help them gain access?

1959

Prime Minister Diefenbaker appoints Georges Vanier Canada's first French-Canadian Governor General.

1960

Aboriginal Peoples win the right to vote in Canada.

Political Leaders
1940s

Thérèse Casgrain

1941	**1942**	**1943**
Canada declares war on Japan.	Prime Minister Mackenzie King announces the removal of all Japanese Canadians residing within 160 kilometres of the Pacific Coast.	Alberta's premier, William Aberhart, dies in office.

Thérèse Casgrain

Between 1916 and 1925, every province in Canada granted women the right to vote except one. That province was Quebec. Thérèse Casgrain decided to change this situation. In 1913, Casgrain organized the Montreal **Suffrage** Association. She campaigned for the vote until April 25, 1940, when Quebec women finally won the right. With this newly won right, Casgrain joined the Cooperative Commonwealth Federation (CCF), a precursor to the New Democratic Party. She was chosen leader of the Quebec wing in 1951. This was the first time a woman was chosen to head a Canadian political party. In 1970, Casgrain was named to the Senate. She died in 1981 at the age of 85.

1940

At the Side of Britain

When World War II broke out in 1939, Prime Minister William Lyon Mackenzie King proclaimed, on a national radio broadcast, that Canada was "at the side of Britain." The first Canadian troops sailed for Great Britain in December 1939. During World War II, Canada contributed food supplies, financial aid, ships, aircraft, and troops to the war effort. More than one million Canadians served in the war,

At the Side of Britain

and about 45,000 died in the effort. In 1942, King faced one of the most difficult issues of his career. This issue was forced military service, or conscription. As the war went on, fewer Canadians volunteered. To keep the number of troops up, King needed to bring in conscription. A national vote was held. It asked Canadians to release the government from its promise not to bring about overseas conscription. King received permission, and in 1944, conscripted troops were sent overseas.

1944

Tommy Douglas

Tommy Douglas entered politics to bring about change in Canada. In 1935, at the height of the **Great Depression**, he ran as a CCF candidate and won a seat in the House of Commons. Douglas argued that the government

should do more to help the average Canadian citizen. In 1944, he resigned his seat in the Commons to run for premier of Saskatchewan. The CCF won 47 of the 53 seats. Douglas became premier, forming the first socialist government in North America. He would hold this position for 17 years. Under his government, labour standards were improved, roads were paved, electricity was brought to the majority of the province, and bills were introduced to protect farmers from foreclosure. One of Douglas's greatest achievements was the introduction of free health care to Saskatchewan. In the years that followed, the federal government adopted this program for the country. Universal health care became available nationwide.

Tommy Douglas

1944

Tommy Douglas becomes premier of Saskatchewan.

1945

Canada plays a key role in the liberation of Holland.

Uncle Louis

In 1948, Louis St. Laurent took over the leadership of the Liberal Party from retiring Mackenzie King. A federal election was called the following year. During the campaign, St. Laurent earned the nickname "Uncle Louis" from the press for his ability to connect with children on the campaign trail. The Liberals won the election with more seats than they had ever won before.

St. Laurent acquired the job of prime minster during the peaceful post-war years. It was a time of economic boom. His main concern as prime minister was national unity. In his first year as prime minister, St. Laurent welcomed Newfoundland into Confederation. He also passed the Trans-Canada Highway Act. This saw the building of 7,821 kilometres of highway from Victoria, British Columbia, to St. John's, Newfoundland. On the world stage, St. Laurent was involved in the creation of the United Nations and the raising of a volunteer army for service with the UN force in the Korean War. St. Laurent retired from politics in 1958.

Uncle Louis

1946

The Canadian racing ship, *Bluenose*, sinks near Haiti.

1947

The Canadian Citizenship Act passes.

1948

Louis St. Laurent of the Liberal party becomes prime minister.

A Modern Father of Confederation

A Modern Father of Confederation

From the early 1900s until 1934, Newfoundland was a dominion of the British Empire. This meant it had the same status as Canada within the British Empire. However, after the Great Depression of the 1930s, Newfoundland was in poor economic shape. It needed help, so Newfoundland's government asked the government of Great Britain if it could be a colony again. Newfoundland's economy strengthened during World War II, and Newfoundland looked to a future free from under British control. The government of Newfoundland decided to hold a referendum to see what the people wanted. They were given three options. Newfoundland could remain a British colony, it could revert to dominion status, or it could become part of Canada. One of the members of the organizing committee for the referendum was Joseph Roberts Smallwood, a journalist, activist, and politician. He argued in favour of joining Canada. Smallwood told his fellow Newfoundlanders that, by becoming the tenth province of Canada, their future would be better. When it came time to vote, however, the results were torn between joining Canada and reverting to dominion status, with no clear majority. A second referendum was called for July. This time, the results were in favour of Confederation. In 1949, Newfoundland became part of Confederation, and Smallwood was elected its first Canadian premier. Smallwood went on to win six provincial elections. He retired from politics in 1972.

Into the Future

Prime ministers of Canada have come from diverse educational backgrounds. Some have studied law. Others have studied political science, economics, history, or sociology. Why is a politician's educational background important? How does it help him or her govern? What type of education do you think a person should have in order to become prime minister? Do you think it is necessary to go to university to become prime minister?

1949

Newfoundland becomes a Canadian province.

1950

Canada participates in the Korean War.

1930s

R. B. Bennett

Bennett's name became identified with anything that did not work. Cars pulled by horses because the owners could no longer afford gasoline were called "Bennett-buggies." Near the end of his term, Bennett proposed a new government platform. He advocated social reforms, such as unemployment insurance, but it was too late. Mackenzie King, using the slogan "King or Chaos," swept to power over Bennett's Conservatives. Bennett remained leader of the opposition until 1938 but later left Canada in 1941 for Great Britain. He never lived in Canada again.

1930

R. B. Bennett

Prime Minister Richard Bedford Bennett governed during the worst days of the Great Depression. The depression years brought high unemployment. People had little food or money.

Many had to rely on government help. Bennett's policies did little to improve the economy. He limited government payments to the unemployed and, instead, sent unemployed men to work camps, where they made as little as 20 cents a day. As the Great Depression worsened, the public became even more frustrated.

1931

The Statute of Westminster allows dominions to independently conduct their external relations.

1932

The CCF is formed in Saskatchewan.

1933

Maurice Duplessis becomes leader of Quebec's Conservatives.

Co-operative Commonwealth Federation

Adrian Arcand

Adrian Arcand

Adrian Arcand was a Montreal journalist and the leader of the National Unity Party. Arcand blamed **communists** and cultural groups for the Great Depression and the worsening unemployment. He called for the deportation of cultural groups to Hudson Bay. In 1939, with World War II looming, Arcand announced his plan to march to Ottawa and take over the country. Instead, he was arrested in Montreal for "plotting to overthrow the state." Arcand was placed in an **internment camp** in New Brunswick for the rest of the war, and his party was declared illegal. He told many people that, one day, he would rule Canada

1932

Co-operative Commonwealth Federation

In the 1930s, drought turned much of Alberta and Saskatchewan into a dust bowl. Crops that could be harvested brought in little money due to low world prices for wheat. Many people were desperate for change. A new political party, the Co-operative Commonwealth Federation, or CCF, became the voice of the disadvantaged and disenchanted. James Shaver Woodsworth, a **pacifist** and activist, was the CCF's first leader. Even before the formation of the CCF, he campaigned ardently on behalf of farmers, immigrants, and workers, recommending that the government create an unemployment insurance program and a government-sponsored old age pension plan. As a member of Parliament, Woodsworth continued to speak out for the common people. He died in 1942, while still in office. Following a 2004 poll, Woodsworth was named one of the top 100 greatest Canadians of all time.

1934

At age 37, Mitchell Hepburn becomes the youngest premier of Ontario in history.

1935

William Aberhart is elected premier of Alberta.

Maurice Duplessis

1935

William "Bible Bill" Aberhart

In the 1930s, many Albertans gathered around their radios to listen to evangelist William "Bible Bill" Aberhart's Sunday broadcast. The program was a blend of religion and politics. Aberhart was both a preacher and member of the Social Credit Party, a political party that believed in sharing wealth. During the Great Depression, this political platform was popular, and Aberhart firmly believed that it was the solution to Alberta's problems. If elected premier, he promised that every adult citizen of Alberta would be given $25 a month. His message was so popular that, in 1935, his party won the provincial election, and Aberhart became premier. However, the provincial treasury did not have enough money to provide the promised funding. Instead, Aberhart and his government decided to print its own money, called "prosperity certificates." In the end, his idea did not work as planned. Manufacturers, retailers, and even government-owned stores refused to accept the prosperity certificates as cash.

1936

Maurice Duplessis

In 1935, Duplessis created the Union Nationale, which was a political party made up of both liberal and conservative politicians. As leader of this party, Duplessis, known as "Le Chef," was elected premier of Quebec from 1936 to 1939 and again from 1944 to 1959. Duplessis focussed much of his attention on education and health care. During his term in office, his government approved the construction of several schools and hospitals. As a champion of French culture, in 1944, his government adopted the fleur-de-lis as the Quebec flag. At the same time, civil liberties decreased under Duplessis. He put into place the Padlock Law. This law allowed the closing of any building suspected of being used to spread communism. Proof was not required. The law was later struck down as unconstitutional by the Supreme Court of Canada. Duplessis died in office in 1959.

William "Bible Bill" Aberhart

1936

Barbara Hanley is elected Canada's first woman mayor.

1937

Ontario's Liberal Party wins its second consecutive majority.

Cairine Reay Wilson

Cairine Reay Wilson

Senator Cairine Reay Wilson was Canada's first female senator. She was appointed to the position in 1930 by William Lyon Mackenzie King. During World War II, many British parents sent their children to Canada to escape the war. Wilson worked with Charlotte Whitton of the Canadian Welfare Council to provide homes for these child war refugees. In 1949, Wilson became the first woman delegate to the United Nations General Assembly. She was also chair of the Canadian National Committee on Refugees. In 1950, Wilson's work with refugee children was recognized when France made her a Knight of the Legion of Honour.

Into the Future

From 1929 until 1939, there was a worldwide economic depression. Canada was deeply affected by the depression. Unemployment was rampant. Many people lost their homes, their farms, and other possessions. They were dependent on government relief for food. During an economic crisis, who is responsible for helping those in need? If you were prime minister during such a crisis, how would you respond to the needs of the country's citizens?

1938	1939	1940
Saskatchewan's Liberal Party wins its second consecutive majority.	Canada declares war on Germany.	Women win the right to vote in Quebec.

Arthur Meighen

1920

Arthur Meighen

Conservative leader Arthur Meighen became Canada's ninth prime minister when Robert Borden retired. As a cabinet minister in the Borden government, Meighen helped nationalize the railways. Meighen had the task of leading the Conservative Party in the 1921 election. The Conservatives had been in power for 10 years but had fallen out of favour after World War I. Meighen's Conservatives lost the election, and Meighen became leader of the opposition. Meighen returned to the prime minister's position in 1926, but his new government lasted only months. It was defeated in the House of Commons with a non-confidence vote. Meighen resigned as leader of the Conservative Party shortly after. Almost 10 years later, in 1942, Meighen attempted a comeback but failed to win a seat in the House of Commons. He then retired from politics.

1921

Agnes Macphail is the first woman to be elected to the House of Commons.

1922

Women in Prince Edward Island win the right to vote.

1923

The Department of National Defence is created.

1921

William Lyon Mackenzie King

William Lyon Mackenzie King was Canada's prime minister for most of the period between 1921 and 1930 and again from 1935 to 1940. In total, King led Canada for almost 22 years. As prime minister in the 1920s, he worked to lower the federal debt. In the 1930s, he signed a trade agreement with the United States and pushed for independence from Great Britain. One of King's most important social policies was introducing the old age pension program in 1926. He tried to help Canadians during the Great Depression by bringing in the unemployment insurance program in 1940 and the Family Allowances Act, which provided growing families with financial support, in 1944. After leading Canada through World War II, King retired from politics in 1948.

William Lyon Mackenzie King

1921

Agnes Macphail

In 1921, Agnes Macphail became the first elected female member of Parliament. For 14 years, Macphail fought for old age pensions, prison reform, and disability pensions. In 1939, she founded the Elizabeth Fry Society of Canada. The society helps women and girls in the justice system. Macphail's influence was felt outside of Canada as well. In 1929, she became the first Canadian woman to be sent as a delegate to the League of Nations in Geneva, Switzerland. One of her final political feats took place in Ontario in 1951, when she championed laws that demanded equal pay for equal work.

Agnes Macphail

1924

The Royal Canadian Air Force is formed.

1925

The women of Newfoundland win the right to vote and hold provincial office.

Irene Parlby

The Alberta Five

1921

Irene Parlby

In 1916, Irene Parlby presented a paper at the United Farm Women of Alberta convention in Calgary entitled *Women's Place in the Nation*. She argued that women should take on various roles in society. Parlby led by example in this argument. She was a president of the United Farm Women of Alberta and ran for the provincial government in 1921. She went on to become the first female cabinet minister in Alberta's history. Serving in the legislature for 14 years, Parlby worked on behalf of women and children to give them better health care. In 1930,

Parlby represented Canada at the League of Nations in Geneva. She was also a member of the "Famous Five," a group of women who petitioned to have women recognized as "persons" under the law.

1928

The Famous Five

In 1928, women could not be appointed to the Senate. This was because, under the law, a woman was not a "person." Five women, Nellie McClung, Emily Murphy, Henrietta Muir Edwards, Louise McKinney, and Irene Parlby, decided to challenge the law. They took their fight to the Supreme Court of Canada, demanding that the

law be changed to acknowledge women as persons. They did not succeed. The Supreme Court ruled that Canadian women were not persons. The women, who later became known as the Famous Five, appealed the decision to the Judicial Committee of the Privy Council in Great Britain, the highest court of appeal for Canada at the time. Here, they were successful. The Privy Council ruled that the word "persons" included men and women. In their decision, they wrote, "The exclusion of women from all public offices is a relic of days more barbarous than ours." Four months later, Prime Minister Mackenzie King appointed the first woman to the Senate, Cairine Reay Wilson.

1926

William Lyon Mackenzie King of the Liberal Party becomes prime minister of Canada.

1927

The Old Age Pensions Act comes into effect.

Idola Saint-Jean

Canadian women gained the right to vote in federal elections in 1918. Most provinces then granted women the right to vote in provincial elections. Quebec, however, was an exception. Idola Saint-Jean, a teacher, felt women should have the right to vote at all levels of government. Male politicians and the clergy saw this as a threat to the traditional family structure. They argued that a woman's place was in the home. In 1927, Saint-Jean founded the Canadian Alliance for Women's Vote in Quebec. From 1927 until 1940, Saint-Jean fought for the right to vote and for women to have access to professional jobs. On April 25, 1940, Quebec women won the right to vote in provincial elections. A plaque celebrating Saint-Jean was unveiled in Montreal in 2002.

Idola Saint-Jean

Into the Future

Throughout the world, Canada is known for its social programs, including old age pensions, unemployment insurance, and universal health care. The country has built its reputation on its concern for the welfare of its citizens. What other types of social programs should Canada develop for its citizens?

1928	1929	1930
The Supreme Court of Canada rules that women are not persons.	The Privy Council rules that women are persons under the law.	R. B. Bennett becomes prime minister.

1910

Henri Bourassa

Henri Bourassa was a journalist and politician who fought for French-Canadian rights. Bourassa was part of Laurier's government, but he left the Liberal Party when he disagreed with Canada's participation in the Boer War in South Africa. For a time, he sat in the House of Commons as an independent, but by 1907, he had left federal politics entirely. Three years later, he founded a newspaper called *Le Devoir*, which became known as the voice of French nationalism. The paper's motto was *Fais ce que dois* or "Do as you must." *Le Devoir* advocated equality for French and English languages in Canada and represented the rights of French

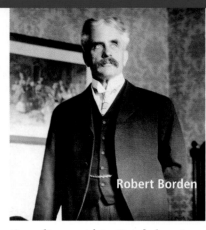

Robert Borden

Canadians within Confederation. Bourassa served as editor of *Le Devoir* until 1932. The paper continues to publish to this day.

1911

Robert Borden

Sir Robert Laird Borden of the Conservative Party served as prime minister from 1911 to 1920. During World War I, Borden imposed conscription to keep the number of Canadian troops high. Under Borden's "selective" conscription plan, unmarried men between the ages of 20 and 34 were conscripted. At the end of the war, Borden felt Canada had grown as a country and no longer needed to be dependent on Great Britain. He felt Canada needed to establish an independent voice internationally. He was successful convincing Great Britain to acknowledge Canada

Henri Bourassa

and its other dominions as equal partners. Defining the relationship in this way eventually led to the British Empire being renamed the British Commonwealth of Nations.

1917

Women's Vote

In 1917, Prime Minister Borden introduced a bill in Parliament giving the right to vote to women relatives of soldiers serving in the armed forces. The decision was not welcomed by all members of Parliament. Some MPs felt this was a ploy to get more votes in the upcoming election. In the December election, Borden's conservatives won a minority government. By 1918, the right to vote was won for most Canadian women 21 years old and over.

1911

Robert Borden becomes prime minister.

1914

Canada formally declares war on Germany.

1915

Nellie McClung presents the Alberta legislature with a petition demanding that women be given the right to vote.

Women's Vote

Frederick Loft and Aboriginal Rights

1919

A Farmer and Politician

Ernest Charles Drury, born in Barrie, Ontario, was a farmer and a politician. His father was Ontario's first minister of agriculture, while Ernest himself was the co-founder and first president of the United Farmers of Ontario (UFO), formed in 1914. The UFO fought for farmers' interests. When the UFO won the provincial election of 1919, Drury saw the election result as an "uprising of the people against the two-party system." Drury's administration reformed the welfare system, providing allowances for widows and children. It also established a minimum wage for women workers. Quickly known as a "people's government," support for the UFO grew across Canada. The party soon became national and was eventually known as the Progressive Party.

1910s

Frederick Loft and Aboriginal Rights

The 1910s were a time of great social progress in Canada, but one sector was not experiencing this advancement. The rights of Canada's Aboriginal Peoples experienced more restrictions than liberation. The Indian Act was responsible for much of this treatment. Under the Indian Act, many Aboriginal customs, including pow-wows, were banned.

The government's goal in implementing these changes was to absorb Canada's Aboriginal Peoples into the mainstream. Frederick Loft, a Mohawk veteran of World War I, decided to challenge this goal. After participating in the war, many Aboriginal veterans felt that they had proven their right to speak for themselves. On September 3, 1919, the first meeting of the National League of Indians was held in Sault Ste. Marie, Ontario. Loft became the league's first president. The league's goals were to gain better access to education for their children and the right to vote. By 1922, the organization became known as the League of Indians of Western Canada. Its representatives hoped that the federal government would be willing to listen to their ideas, but instead, it had the opposite reaction. In 1927, the government silenced the league by making it illegal to raise funds to "pursue any aboriginal rights." Aboriginal Canadians had to wait until 1960 for the right to vote in federal elections.

A Farmer and Politician

1916

Manitoba becomes the first Canadian province to grant women the right to vote.

1920

Canada is a founding member of the League of Nations.

Political Leaders
1900s

Wilfrid Laurier

1900s

Wilfrid Laurier

Sir Wilfrid Laurier, the first French Canadian prime minister, came to power in 1896. He remained prime minister for 15 years. The Laurier years were prosperous for Canada. Trade increased, and Canada's natural resources were developed. Under Laurier, immigration boomed, the railway expanded, and two new provinces, Saskatchewan and Alberta, were created.

1900s

External Affairs

Laurier wanted Canada to be respected in the world. This would happen only if Canada had greater control over its relationship with world governments. Laurier created the Department of External Affairs to further this end, but it would take years before Canada had its own foreign policy. Instead, Laurier worked at building and strengthening relationships with key countries.

He showed Canada's support of Great Britain by agreeing to send troops to South Africa during the Boer War. He also worked on improving Canada-U.S. relations. Laurier believed that Canada could be a strong independent nation, standing on its own. For 15 years, Canadians believed in him. Laurier eventually fell from power, but stayed on as leader of the opposition after he was defeated. In this role, Laurier spoke up for French language rights and against forced military service.

1900

1902

r designates
ay.

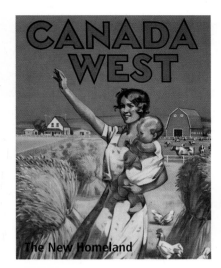
The New Homeland

The New Homeland

Clifford Sifton, Canada's minister of the interior, was a great supporter of Canadian agriculture. He often said that agriculture was Canada's most valuable resource as it feeds the population "...which is the backbone of a nation." Sifton believed that the way to develop the country's agricultural resources was through immigration. Sifton had a major impact on Canadian immigration in the 1900s. He allowed immigrants to secure their homesteads quickly and eliminated the land grant system that allowed railway companies to hold agricultural land. Sifton campaigned in Great Britain, the United States, and Europe for immigrants. He advertised Canada's frontier as "the last, best West." "Homes for Millions," posters declared. His advertising worked. Between 1896 and 1898, immigration to Canada doubled. More than 170,000 Ukrainian settlers came to Canada, while thousands more arrived from the United States. Other people moved to Canada from Scandinavia, Hungary, Germany, and Poland. Sifton retired in 1911. He was knighted in 1915 by King George V.

1908

Nellie McClung

In the 1900s, the Dominion Elections Act stated that "no woman, idiot, lunatic, or criminal shall vote." Many women in the 1900s believed that they should be allowed to vote. These women were called suffragists. Women's suffrage was not popular with all Canadians. Many politicians were against it. Some believed that suffrage would lead to the breakdown of the family. It was even argued that women were less intelligent than men. Nellie McClung was a suffragist and a founding member of the Political Equality League. The league held a mock parliament on January 28, 1914, in order to rally public support for women's suffrage. McClung acted as premier. The mock parliament was a success. On January 29, Manitoba became the first Canadian province to grant women the right to vote.

1900s

United Farmers of Alberta

In the 1900s, co-operative farming organizations formed in Canada. Farmers felt the need to organize so they could gain greater control over their produce. Often, farmers in the West found it hard to earn a living. High taxes and transportation costs often exceeded the value of their crops. The United Farmers of Alberta (UFA) was formed out of this need to make farmers' voices heard and encourage reforms. Fair prices for goods and affordable transportation were two of the UFA's goals. Over time, the UFA became a political party. It formed the government in Alberta from 1921 until 1935. At its height, the UFA had more than 30,000 members and 1,200 local clubs.

Nellie McClung

United Farmers of Alberta

1905
Alexander Rutherford becomes

1908
Laurier wins fourth

1910
Henri Bourassa founds the

ACTIVITY
Into the Future

Leaders use their influence to bring about change. Training, education, and experience are some of the essentials to becoming a good leader. Communication is also key. Good leaders encourage communication. They listen to what people have to say.

Internationally, federally, provincially, and at the municipal level, decisions made by leaders affect your life. Even decisions made in your own school affect you. Your principal, your teachers, and your student council all make decisions that impact you. Think about some of the issues facing your school. Is there a situation that you feel needs to be addressed, such as healthier food in the cafeteria or recycling programs? If you can think of ways to improve school life and bring about change, you are on your way to becoming a leader.

Decide what your goals are. How can they be achieved? How can you build and use a team to realize your goal? Answering these questions is the first step toward developing your own platform.

Become a Leader

Start planning a campaign to achieve your goal. Pick a group of friends to work on your campaign committee. Next, create a poster and commercial for your campaign. Think of a campaign slogan that will sum up your ideas. Talk about your platform with friends, and see if they can suggest ways for you to improve it. When your plan is complete, take the necessary steps to launch your campaign.

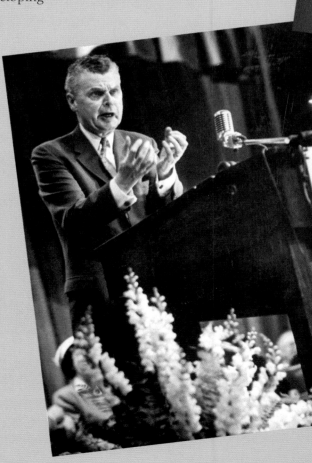

FURTHER
Research

Many books and websites provide information on Canada's political leaders. To learn more about this topic, borrow books from the library, or surf the Internet.

Books

Most libraries have computers that connect to a database for researching information. If you input a key word, you will be provided with a list of books in the library that contain information on that topic. Nonfiction books are arranged numerically, using their call number. Fiction books are organized alphabetically by the author's last name.

Websites

To learn more about the prime ministers of Canada, visit **www.collectionscanada.gc.ca/primeministers/index-e.html**.

For additional information about Canadian history, see **www.canadahistory.com/Index.htm**

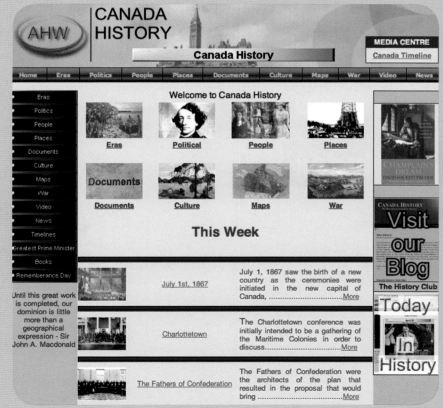

Glossary

assimilation: the absorption of a minority culture into the cultural mainstream

civil liberties: fundamental individual rights, such as freedom of speech and religion, protected by law against unwarranted governmental interference

civil rights: the rights of a citizen of a country

communists: people who support an economic and social system in which property and goods are owned by the government and shared by citizens

Confederation: the joining of Ontario, Quebec, Nova Scotia, and New Brunswick to form Canada

Crown corporations: companies established and regulated by a country's government

democratic: based on the concept that government is run by the people

dominion: a territory or country under the control of another

federalist: a person who believes that government power should be divided between a central authority and regional governments

G20: a group of finance ministers and bank governors from 20 countries

Great Depression: a period of financial decline in the 1920s and 1930s

internment camp: a camp for prisoners of war

nationalist: a movement toward independence of a country or other political entity

NATO: North Atlantic Treaty Organization; a military defence alliance of Western nations

official opposition: the political party that receives the second-highest number of votes in an election

pacifist: someone who is opposed to violence as a means of resolving disputes

patronage: giving out jobs and power positions to friends or supporters

platform: the principles of a political party

portfolio: the office of a cabinet minister

referendum: submitting a matter to a vote

separatist: a person who believes Quebec should be a separate country from Canada

shadow cabinet: those members of the opposition party who function as unofficial counterpart to the cabinet ministers of the party in power

sovereignty: supreme and unrestricted power as a state

suffrage: the right to vote

Index